Half-Truths &
One-and-a-Half Truths

Karl Kraus, 1926

Half-Truths &
One-and-a-Half Truths

kraus
karl

SELECTED APHORISMS

Edited and translated by
HARRY ZOHN

CARCANET

Original publication by Engendra Press Ltd., Montreal, 1976

First published by CARCANET PRESS LIMITED in 1986
208-212 Corn Exchange, Manchester M4 3BQ, UK
108 East 31st Street, New York, NY 10016, USA

"Werke" by Karl Kraus are published in German under the
editorship of Heinrich Fischer
Copyright © Kösel-Verlag GmbH & Co., Munich

Translation & Introduction
Copyright © 1976, 1986 by Harry Zohn

British Library Cataloguing in Publication Data
Kraus, Karl
Half-truths and one-and-a-half truths.
1. Aphorisms and apothegms
I. Title
839'.90202   PT2621.292/

ISBN 0-85635-580-1

The Publisher acknowledges the financial assistance of
the Arts Council of Great Britain.

Printed by SRP Ltd., Exeter

To the memory of

Robert Stolz

Contents

Karl Kraus: An Introduction

"When the age died by its own hand, he was that hand."

Thus did Bertolt Brecht sum up the achievement of Karl Kraus (1874–1936), the vitriolic Viennese satirist who hauled the powerful and the pitiful alike before the tribunal of his satire and who grew to be a legend in his own lifetime, adored or vilified by his contemporaries. It is only of late that Kraus's significance has come to be recognized in the English-speaking world; various articles and books of recent date have focused critical attention on this satirist's accomplishments, lending credibility thereby to Kraus's *Spruch* (dictum) or *Widerspruch* (contradiction), "I have to wait until my writings are obsolete; then they may acquire timeliness."

Merely the smallest fraction of Kraus's extensive output has appeared in English translation, however, and this primarily for two reasons: first, much of his writing is so firmly rooted in the passing scene of his Europe or his Vienna that its intelligibility for today's reader would be slight without an abundance of explanatory matter; second and more important, "Kraus did not," in Erich Heller's words, "write 'in a language,' but through him the beauty, profundity, and accumulated moral experience of the German language assumed personal shape and became the crucial witness in the case this inspired prosecutor brought against his time."[1] Kraus's timeliness (and, at long last, his *relative* exportability and translatability) derive at least in part from certain parallels between his era and ours, and from the need of our age for his vibrant pacifism, his kind of defense of the spirit against dehumanizing tendencies, and his "linguistic-moral imperative" which equates purity of language with purity of thought, with a return to the sources of spiritual strength, and with steadfastness of moral purpose. It is the aim of the present volume to set before English readers a mosaic of Karl Kraus's views, attitudes, and ideas as he disclosed them in aphoristic form, a manner of expression in which Kraus has few peers among modern authors.

Karl Kraus was born the son of a well-to-do manufacturer on 28 April 1874 at Jičín, a small Bohemian town northeast of Prague. Three years later the family moved to Vienna, where Kraus was to spend the rest of his life and with which city he—like his contemporary Sigmund Freud—had a love-hate relationship. His was a family situation not untypical of the turn of the century, one in which the sons of Central European Jewish businessmen—often self-made men who headed patriarchally organized families—rejected the family

1. Erich Heller, "Karl Kraus," in *The Disinherited Mind* (New York: Farrar, Straus & Cudahy, 1957), p. 239.

business in favor of a literary career. Franz Kafka, Stefan Zweig and Franz Werfel, among others, joined Kraus in selecting this path.

Having attended the University of Vienna without taking a degree, Kraus opted for a career on the stage. His shortcomings as an actor, however, turned him irrevocably to journalism and literature, though his talents for mimicry and parody were to find ample expression in later public readings. Indeed, Kraus said of himself that he was perhaps the first author to experience his writings as an actor; an aphorism included in this volume refers to the author's literary work as "written acting."

In 1892 Kraus began to contribute theater criticism, book reviews and other prose pieces to a variety of newspapers and periodicals. He later confessed that his youthful Storm-and-Stress period took the form of cultivating journalistic and literary "connections" with a view to earning a living within the framework of liberal journalism. In his twenties, however, the satirical impulse waxed too warm for accommodation of any sort, and Kraus rejected the prospect of becoming a kind of "culture clown" absorbed by a deceptively effete, slack and *gemütlich* environment, and being accorded, as he put it, "the accursed popularity which a grinning Vienna bestows." Because work within the Establishment seemed to be hedged in with multifarious taboos and considerations of a personal and commercial nature, Kraus turned down a job offer from the *Neue Freie Presse*—Vienna's most prestigious daily— and founded his own journal, *Die Fackel* (The Torch), the first issue of which appeared on 1 April 1899.

The *Fackel* turned out to be as long-lived as it was aggressive. Setting out to "drain a swamp of clichés," Kraus at first enlisted the services of numerous writers and artists—Heinrich Mann, August Strindberg and Oskar Kokoschka, to name but three—though these never contributed more than roughly one-third of the magazine's contents. From 1911 to 1936 the periodical contained Kraus's writings exclusively: "I no longer have collaborators," he wrote. "I used to be envious of them. They repel those readers whom I want to lose myself." The statement is indicative of the uncompromising nature of the unique satirical journal in which Kraus effectively clipped his era and put it between quotation marks. Quotation was the hallmark of Kraus's satire, and in its use he was guided by the insight that what was most unspeakable about his age could be spoken only by the age itself.

The thirty-seven volumes of the *Fackel* (reissued in facsimile form in recent years) are the fruit of a gargantuan effort to fashion the imperishable profile of an age from such highly perishable material as newspaper reports. They contain the bulk of Kraus's literary output; most of the satirist's publications in book form represent distillations from the *Fackel*'s pages. The journal is an enormous pillory, a running autobiography, and an inimitably personal history of Austrian affairs. The small-format *Fackel* had an extraordinary satirical *genius loci*; matters that might have attracted limited attention elsewhere took on heightened relevance when they made their appearance in its pages, and "little people" there achieved "greatness." Thus Kraus's periodical continued to have a good many contributors, albeit unwilling and unwitting ones. It was one journal that never tried to please its readers; Kraus, in fact, was moved to write that "one of the most disagreeable concomitants of the *Fackel* is its readership." J. P. Stern has attempted to assess the *Fackel*'s significance and uniqueness as follows:

> To delimit the intellectual region in which to place this journal, one would have to think of Péguy minus his Catholicism and patriotism; of F. R. Leavis uninvolved in any educational "establishment" plus genius; of the satirist in George Bernard Shaw as milk-and-water to Kraus's vitriol; of the early Wittgenstein's equation of "language" and world; of H. L. Mencken's criticism of the leisure class; of the poet Siegfried Sassoon's "scarlet major at the base"; of the early Evelyn Waugh's type-casting— and all this would have to be translated into the peculiar medium of Vienna.[2]

Kraus began to write when a century top-heavy with historical and cultural events and innovations was approaching its end. In the specific case of his homeland —which was both the source and the target of his satire —the Hapsburg dynasty, worn out after a reign of over six hundred years, was coming to a close along with Austria-Hungary, the political constellation of its last five decades. The reign of Emperor Franz Josef, a man whom Kraus came to attack and lampoon as "the

2. J. P. Stern, "Karl Kraus's Vision of Language," *Modern Language Review* 61 (1966): 73.

Hapsburg demon incarnate," spanned almost seventy years and witnessed the slow and inevitable dissolution of an old political, social, and cultural structure. It was a time of overrefinement and overripeness to the point of decay and death, and Kraus's marked apocalyptic sense and stance as a "late" warner derive in great measure from his epoch's *Zeitgeist*: transitoriness, disintegration, and inner insecurity. Ironically, the satirist shared his initials with Imperial-Royal Austria, the *kaiserlich-königlich* empire, designated by K.K. ("Kah-Kah" in German)—a country which Robert Musil in his novel *The Man Without Qualities* called "Kakanien," or "Kakania." Kraus came to regard this centrally located empire as a "proving ground for world destruction"; his prewar writings constitute variations on this major theme, exposing and satirizing many of the uglier features of Austrian life and culture. From prison conditions to the financial plight of civil servants, Kraus held up to ridicule all that he found noxious, perceiving the seeds of European disintegration in what to others might have seemed local and inconsequential phenomena.

Kraus's first satirical work of importance, *Die demolirte Literatur* (A Literature Demolished), was a witty diatribe about the razing of a Viennese café frequented by literati. The following year saw him produce the pamphlet *Eine Krone für Zion* (A Crown for Zion, 1898) in which he lampoons political Zionism from the standpoint of an assimilated European Jew sympathetic with the cause of socialism. Kraus's Jewishness and his own attitude toward it are problematic. The man has been called everything from "a shining example of Jewish self-hatred" to "an arch-Jew."[3] His writings provide a foundation for both these judgments. Although over the years his efforts to disassociate himself from what he believed to be the negative fruits of modern Judaism led Kraus to make statements overtly anti-Semitic in character, much of his work lends strong support to the view of Frank Field that Kraus's Jewishness is "of vital importance in understanding the particular extremism and sense of the apocalyptic which pervades his work" and that Kraus "attacked his own people in the same way that the prophets of the Old Testament castigated the unworthiness of the Israelites for the trust which God had placed in them."[4] After leaving the Jewish fold in 1899 and remaining *konfessionslos* (religiously unaffiliated) for some years, Kraus secretly converted to Catholicism in 1911, only to leave the Catholic church eleven years later in protest against what he regarded as its unwholesome participation in pseudo-artistic and touristic aspects of the Salzburg Festival. What must above all be borne in mind is that the man who once noted that according to the census Vienna had 2,030,834 inhabitants—"that is, 2,030,833 souls and myself"—refused to be identi-

3. Theodor Lessing, *Der jüdische Selbsthass* (Berlin: Jüdischer Verlag, 1930), p. 43; and Berthold Viertel, "Karl Kraus. Ein Charakter und die Zeit," in *Dichtungen und Dokumente* (Munich: Kösel, 1956), p. 259.
4. Frank Field, *The Last Days of Mankind: Karl Kraus and His Vienna* (New York: St. Martin's Press; London: Macmillan & Co., 1967), p. 68.

fied with *any* ethnic, political or social group.

Of the two women who figured prominently in Kraus's life and writings, the first, Annie Kalmar, a young actress who died in 1901 of tuberculosis, had a profound—and posthumous—influence on the moralist's early thought. The young woman's association with Kraus occasioned a scurrilous attack on her in a Viennese paper after her death, a libel that opened the satirist's eyes to the perverse standards of sexual morality entertained by contemporary Austria. Thus was a major theme of Kraus's earlier work born, and the second period of his creativity may be dated from the appearance of the essay "Sittlichkeit und Kriminalität" (Morality and Criminal Justice) in 1902. The essay became the title piece of a book-length collection issued six years later in which Kraus concerned himself, on the basis of court cases, with the glaring contrast between private and public morality and with the hypocrisy inherent in the administration of justice in Austria.

In turning a powerful spotlight on a male-dominated society with its double standards, its shameless encroachment on privacy and its sensation-mongering press, Kraus expressed not a few ideas and attitudes germane to such present-day issues as women's rights, child abuse, sexual mores, and even "gay liberation." The gloomy, bitter wit of this collection gave way to a lighter brand of humor in Kraus's next book, *Die chinesische Mauer* (The Great Wall of China), which went through five editions between 1910 and 1930. Kraus's bitterness was far from having run its course, however: writing on Peary's discovery of the North Pole in 1909, he could remark with old-time acerbity

—and with awful prescience—that "progress celebrates Pyrrhic victories over nature" and that it "makes purses out of human skin."

The other woman of great importance to Kraus was the Baroness Sidonie Nádherný, a Czech aristocrat to whom Kraus proposed marriage more than once between 1913 and 1915 and by whom he was consistently turned down, partly on the strength of the poet Rilke's counsel. The relationship (the source of much of Kraus's poetry and many of his aphorisms on the subject of women) remained warm until the satirist's death. Kraus's more than a thousand letters and postcards to the Baroness, long thought lost, were rediscovered in 1969 and recently published in Germany. The collection is of interest for its almost overwhelming presentation of an emotional side of Kraus not hitherto revealed to the public.

It should be noted that despite Kraus's attack on the double standard of sexual morality, he by no means saw men and women as identical beings: in tune with certain ideas in the air at the time and drawing conviction from personal relationships, Kraus saw man as a creature strong in intellect and imagination while wanting in emotional capacity, and women as sensuous, intellectually flaccid, and irrational. In time Kraus came to extol what he thought of as female qualities, however, finding in them a much-needed antidote to man's innate rationalism which he believed to be at the root of his contemporaries' unhealthy respect for science and technology.

Kraus engaged in unremitting satirical warfare against the press, a struggle motivated by his view of journalism as a vast switchboard that concentrated and activated the forces of corruption, dissolution and decay. Recognizing a disturbing identity between *Zeit* and *Zeitung*, his age and the newspapers it spawned, with *Worte* (words) usurping and destroying *Werte* (values), and news reports causing as well as describing actions and events, he had visions of the destruction of the world by the black magic of printer's ink (*Untergang der Welt durch schwarze Magie* is the title of a collection issued in 1922 and made up of material from the prewar *Fackel*). Kraus once expressed the wish that everything could be printed in the *Neue Freie Presse* so that he might concentrate his fire and, God-like, rest on the seventh day. (That liberal paper, referred to by more than one commentator as the *New York Times* of its day, together with its longtime editor Moriz Benedikt—or "Maledikt"—was a prime target of Kraus's satire.) Kraus was convinced that the moving forces of his time were entrenched not in parliaments but in editorial offices, controlling capital and the government, influencing public opinion as well as the arts and sciences, and killing thought, taste, and imagination. Decades before Hermann Hesse coined the phrase "das feuilletonistische Zeitalter" in his utopian novel *The Glass Bead Game*, Kraus recognized his era as "the age of the feuilleton" in which newspaper accounts took precedence over events, form eclipsed substance, and the style, the atmosphere, the "package" were all-important. The press, that "goiter of the world," was seen as the polluter of language and poisoner of the human spirit. In his polemical essay *Heine und die Folgen* (Heine and the Consequences, 1910), Kraus excoriated the nineteenth-century German-Jewish poet and essayist for introducing the feuilleton in Germany and providing an inheritance on which journalism has drawn to this day: its function as a dangerous intermediary between art and life and as a parasite on both, creating a deleterious, linguistically deceitful mixture of intellect and information, reportage and literature.

The outbreak of the war in 1914 marked a turning point in Kraus's life and creativity, and the outraged convictions of the pacifist and moralist inspired him to produce his most powerful and most characteristic work. Following several months of silence, Kraus delivered, on 19 November, a sardonic public lecture, "In these great times . . .," which may be regarded as the germ cell of his extensive wartime output. Kraus set himself up as the lonely, bold, inexorable chronicler of what he termed "the last days of mankind" and "the Day of Judgment" for the benefit of a posterity that might no longer inhabit this planet. "What is at stake in the war," wrote Kraus, "is the life or death of language." It goes without saying that he was shocked by the enormous loss of human lives, including those of several of his beloved and admired relatives, fellow writers, and friends. Kraus saw the war as the tragedy of mankind enacted by figures with all the stature, substance and truthfulness of characters in an operetta. Without waiting for the detachment that time might have brought him, Kraus wrote the 209 scenes of the 5 acts of *Die letzten Tage der Menschheit* (The Last Days of Mankind) as well as the 10-scene Prologue and the

Epilogue between July 1915 and July 1917. The first version of the play appeared in several special issues of the *Fackel*, and parts of it were read by Kraus at a number of wartime recitals, censorship apparently having been but a minor problem in that era. In Kraus's lifetime only the Epilogue—"The Last Night"—was performed in a special stage version; after World War II, however, Heinrich Fischer, a close associate of Kraus and his onetime literary executor, and Leopold Lindtberg prepared an abridged version of the drama (in its entirety it runs to almost 800 printed pages) which was seen on the stage and televised in Europe.

The Last Days of Mankind, originally subtitled "Ein Angsttraum" (A Nightmare), begins with the voice of a newsboy and ends with the voice of God. Its setting is "a hundred scenes and hells," the streets of Vienna and Berlin, offices and army barracks, churches and cafés, places of amusement and military hospitals, railroad stations and army posts. The play's many hundreds of characters include poets and prostitutes, professors and politicians, teachers and tradesmen, soldiers and sycophants, children and churchmen, journalists and jesters, editors and emperors. There are many actual as well as fictitious persons, and through their authentic speech patterns they reveal and judge themselves. Kraus attempts—as Max Spalter has pointed out—to make language the moral index of a dying way of life; in an enormous phonomontage "a world literally talks its way to perdition."[5]

5. Max Spalter, *Brecht's Tradition* (Baltimore: Johns Hopkins Press, 1967), p. 149.

This dramatic typology of man's inhumanity to man, basically documentary in character, is a striking amalgam of naturalistic and symbolic elements. The scenes are by turn lyrical and prosaic, comic and tragic; even what seems to be lighthearted and purely humorous, however, tends to acquire a certain grimness from its context and results in gallows humor. There is no humor or plot in the conventional Aristotelian sense. The scenes range in length from one-line "black-outs" in the tradition of the cabaret (more often than not, what gets blacked out is the human spirit) to lengthy dialogues, dramatized editorials, and phantasmagoric tableaux. Kraus's wartime waxworks of "Goethe's people" and his fellow Austrians include such characters as the two fatuous privy councillors who vie with each other in mangling Goethe's "Wanderer's Nightsong," one of the glories of German poetry; the Bavarian storyteller Ludwig Ganghofer who yodels his way along the front, writes war reports for the *Neue Freie Presse* and swaps jokes with an appreciative Kaiser; "patriotic" pastors of the "praise-the-Lord-and-pass-the-ammunition" variety who bear the names of birds of prey; and Alice Schalek, the first woman accredited to the Austrian army as a correspondent, whose gushy effusions in denatured language about the "common man," the "liberated human spirit" and the "fervor of experiencing," and whose search for "human-interest" material amidst degradation, destruction and death made her a macabre joke and a frequent target of Kraus's satire. As the tragedy rushes toward its cataclysmic conclusion, surrealistic touches are introduced: "Corybants and Maenads" spew forth word fragments;

and Gas Masks, Frozen Soldiers, 1200 Drowned Horses, and the Doomed Children of the *Lusitania* deliver choruses. The rhymed Epilogue is a harrowing poetic satire raised to a supernatural plane in which many of the play's motifs are recapitulated in cinematographic or operatic form. And finally, breaking the silence that follows utter destruction, God's voice is heard to echo the words attributed to Kaiser Wilhelm at the war's beginning: "Ich habe es nicht gewollt" (This was not my will).

The story of Kraus's postwar writings and polemics is essentially the history of his disillusionment as his "homeland's loyal hater." The best that Kraus could find to say about the Austrian Republic, which was still bedevilled by "the parasites remaining from the imperial age and the blackheads of the revolution," was that it had replaced the monarchy and rid Karl Kraus of "that burdensome companion, the other K.K." In a poem entitled "Here in This Land,"[6] Kraus described his situation and pinpointed what impeded his full effectiveness.

**Here in this land no one is deemed absurd
but who should speak the truth. And all defenseless
he stands before the sneering, grinning herd,
which holds a sense of honor senseless.**

6. The translation is that of Albert Bloch in *Karl Kraus: Poems* (Boston: Four Seas Co., 1930), p. 106. Mrs. Anna Francis Bloch has graciously consented to its reproduction in this context.

Here in this land, where God is bought and sold
and manhood is pursued with execration,
all infamy is coined to purest gold
and lords it high in honor's station.

Here in this land you run a gauntlet's lane
of cut-purses who fervently despise you
and either get your purse by some chicane
or pat your back to show they prize you.

Here in this land, whatever be your boast,
you are not master of your own decision.
The pest of greed obtrudes by every post,
effectively to blight your vision.

Here in this land you beat the empty air
would you denounce one evil or another,
and every grinning rascal debonair
in this land hails you as his brother.

Among those with whom Kraus engaged in extended
polemics over the years may be mentioned the German-Jewish publicist Maximilian Harden and the
Prague-born poet, novelist and dramatist Franz Werfel, the two being typical in that Kraus's opponents
had frequently been either great admirers of Kraus or
greatly admired by him. Another apostle turned
apostate was the psychoanalyst Fritz Wittels who presented a paper on "The *Fackel* Neurosis" at a meeting
of the Vienna Psychoanalytic Society. Sigmund Freud
had at one time been in touch with Kraus, perhaps
seeing in him a kindred spirit, but his efforts to estab-

lish a fruitful line of communication with the satirist
came to naught. Wittels's paper constituted something
of a counteroffensive against the potshots that Kraus
was wont to direct at the practice of analysis and
psychoanalysts generally. While he may have had some
respect for the pioneering spirit of Freud himself,
Kraus's tolerance of the man's followers and the nonsense they expounded in the name of science was nil.
Kraus was convinced that the "psychoanals" were doing
their part to crush the human spirit, largely through
their forays into the realm of art criticism, and his
sword-crossing with the analysts was a lengthy affair.

In the middle and late twenties Kraus castigated the
unholy alliance between a police chief named Johannes
Schober and a corrupt press boss named Imre Békessy.
Prevailing against a clique and a claque, Kraus almost
single-handedly waged a spirited and protracted fight
to "kick the crook out of Vienna" ("Hinaus aus Wien
mit dem Schuft" was his ringing slogan), and his cam-
paign bore fruit in the summer of 1926 when Békessy
fled the city. The literary result of the Schober-Békessy
affair was another documentary drama, *Die Unüber-
windlichen* (The Unconquerables), which premiered in
1929. "Once again, as in the last days of a mankind
whose mysterious continued existence has now given
us these scenes," wrote Kraus in his preface, "docu-
ments have become figures, reports have materialized
as forms, and clichés stand on two legs." Other plays
written in the twenties include *Wolkenkuckucksheim*
(Cloudcuckooland), a verse play based on Aristophanes
and presenting a sort of "Last Days of Birdkind," but
with a Shakespearian solo by the Lark at the end
promising conciliation and peace.

Kraus's public readings of his own works and those of others must be regarded as an integral part of his creativity and perhaps even as the apogee of his effectiveness. Following a few early readings in 1892, between 1910 and 1936 Kraus presented 700 recitals in many European cities, with the proceeds often going to charitable causes. After 1925 Kraus used "Theater der Dichtung" (Theater of Poetry, or Literary Theater) as a subheading, reading poetry, prose, and entire plays to large audiences in spellbinding one-man shows— correctives to the overgrown theatrical spectacles of his time. Kraus may be credited with the modern revival of interest in the nineteenth-century Viennese playwright and actor Johann Nestroy, whose works he adapted and presented to show Nestroy in his full stature as a powerful social satirist and a linguistic genius. Kraus often added *Zeitstrophen*, topical stanzas of his own creation, to the songs in Nestroy's comedies. Shakespeare also was a living force in Kraus's life. Between 1916 and 1936 Kraus recited his adaptations of thirteen dramas of the Bard; he also published two collections of plays and the *Sonnets* in his translation. Kraus knew little English, and was guided, in fashioning his own versions from existing translations, by his superior poetic sense and unerring linguistic instinct. Since his unfamiliarity with the original prevented him from achieving literalness, Kraus must have felt that he owed fidelity to the spirit rather than to the letter of the original text. Another figure worthy of mention in this context is Jacques Offenbach, whose work Kraus had admired from his boyhood. He adapted and performed, with a piano accompanist, many of Offenbach's operettas, whose *esprit*, enchanting wit, and telling social satire he appreciated in programmatic contrast to the Viennese operetta of his time (that of Franz Lehár and Emmerich Kálmán, among others) which Kraus regarded as inane, meretricious, false, and unwholesome.

"Mir fällt zu Hitler nichts ein"—Concerning Hitler I cannot think of anything to say. This is the striking first sentence of Kraus's work *Die Dritte Walpurgisnacht* (The Third Walpurgis Night—the title refers to both parts of Goethe's *Faust* as well as to the Third Reich), written in the late spring and summer of 1933 but not published in its entirety during Kraus's lifetime. That sentence, the root of the misunderstandings and conflicts which marked Kraus's last years, may be indicative of resignation (though Kraus *could* think of many things to say about Hitler and did indeed say them) but it is also a hyperbolic, heuristic device for depicting the witches' sabbath of the time. There had been no *Fackel* for ten months when no. 888 appeared in October 1933. Its four pages contained no more than Kraus's funeral oration on his friend the architect Adolf Loos, and what was to be the satirist's last poem, with its poignant closing line, "Das Wort entschlief, als jene Welt erwachte" (The word expired when that world awoke). Karl Kraus was a fundamentally apolitical man with an *ad hoc* attitude toward politics based on personalities rather than parties. "I am a member of no party," he had written in 1931, "but view them all with disdain." And though he supported the Social Democrats at various times in his life, that party—which held a majority position in postwar Austria—grew increasingly annoyed by what it took to be Kraus's deficient understanding of economics, his blindness to the achievements and promises of modern technology, and his carping criticism. But in 1933 Kraus sadly realized the incommensurability of the human spirit with the unspeakably brutal and mindless power structure across the German border. "Is that which has been done to the spirit still a concern of the spirit?" was his anguished question. And the equally anguished reply he himself furnished was: "Force is no object of polemics, madness no object of satire."

Once again language was in mortal danger (Kraus's remarks on this subject anticipate and confirm the dictionaries of the language of inhumanity and the murderers' lexica which appeared after the end of Hitler's self-styled "Thousand-Year Reich"), and the perpetrators of the new horrors obviously were *not* characters from an operetta. As Kraus attempts to deal with the early excesses of the Nazi regime—which led him to foresee much of the full fury to come—he seems to be engaging in a desperate rearguard action; his writing is the rambling monologue of the worried man who talks incessantly in an effort to keep the demons at bay. In voicing genuine concern over Germany's pressure on his homeland, Kraus for once found himself in Austria's corner. Paradoxically, this led him to side with the clerico-fascist regime of Chancellor Dollfuss, whose assassination in 1934 came as a severe shock and blow to Kraus. Many of the satirist's erstwhile leftist adherents, some of them now Communists or emigrants or both, expected Kraus to join them in their struggle against Hitlerism, but they were disappointed by what they regarded as his equivocation.

The *Fackel* lost many readers, and Kraus was content to reduce his readership to those who not only heard "the trumpets of the day" but who were also interested in Shakespeare, Nestroy, Offenbach, and German style, including Kraus's unique "comma problems." Kraus prepared to "live in the safe sentence structure," as he put it, and tried—pathetically and futilely—to pit the word against the sword. His death of heart failure on 12 June 1936 following a long period of physical and spiritual exhaustion mercifully saved him from witnessing the Nazi take-over of Austria to the cheers of most of its population, and—among other horrors—the destruction of his belongings and the deaths of close friends in concentration camps. "In the twelve years that followed the accession of Hitler to power in Germany," writes Frank Field, "things were to happen that surpassed the most pessimistic insights of the satirist: the building of the concentration camp at Buchenwald around Goethe's beech tree, and the processions that took place into the extermination chambers of Auschwitz while elsewhere in the camp the orchestra played selections from Viennese light music—all this only becomes a little more explicable after reading the works of Kraus."[7]

Apart from the importance of the timeless humanitarian ideals that Kraus espoused, the relevance of his satire to our age is readily apparent. So astute an observer of the Israeli scene as Robert Weltsch has re-

7. Field, p. 212.

marked that in the Yom Kippur War of 1973 "there was no shortage of the sort of reporting which has become a modern feature—and a matter of disgust—since the First World War, and to which Karl Kraus has set a monument."[8] It is not difficult to imagine what Kraus would have had to say about the "Newspeak" of our day, about the denatured language of contemporary politicking, a language designed to conceal, not reveal, human thought, or about the "Doublethink" in Orwell's *1984*. Surely there is a parallel between Alice Schalek's use of the word *ausputzen* (clean out) in connection with enemy trenches, or the Viennese vulgarism *obidraht* for a similar act, and our soldiery's "waste" or "off" as euphemisms for "kill." And our linguistically permissive age, an era which, as Marshall McLuhan puts it, tends to "bypass language in favor of a general cosmic consciousness," is as "language-forsaken" as Kraus's time. Robert Lilienfeld, finally, has drawn our attention to the incontrovertible fact that the unconquerables are back and that Kraus would not fail to recognize them. "In his time," Lilienfeld writes, "he could track them down and uncover their lies, for they had only the press; but now they have not only the press but radio, television, films, and the universities."[9] Surely the fact that there is no Karl Kraus today to do battle with the polluters of language and the defilers of the human spirit is part of the sadness of our time.

8. Robert Weltsch, "Where Do We Go From Here? Reflections on the Yom Kippur War," *AJR Information* (London) 28, no. 12 (December 1973): 1.

9. Robert Lilienfeld, "Reflections on Karl Kraus—Part II," *The Nation*, 30 April 1973, p. 572.

"Meine Sprache ist die Allerweltshure, die ich zur Jungfrau mache" (My language is the common prostitute that I turn into a virgin). This aphorism illuminates both Kraus's mission and his method. While many poets have striven to restore pristine purity to a language and make of it once more a serviceable vehicle for poetic expression, Kraus's obsession with language went considerably beyond such a pursuit. As Heinrich Fischer has pointed out, Kraus was "one of the most marked egocentrics of art, filled with a metaphysical compulsion to trace in himself the divine and intellectual center of language and represent it through himself."[10] He saw an absolute congruity between word and world, language and life; the unworthiness of his age was for him defined by its treatment of language. Kraus never tired of emphasizing the connection between language and morality; in his eyes language was the moral criterion and accreditation for a writer or speaker. J. P. Stern, to be sure, suspects that what he has called Kraus's "moral-linguistic imperative," his equation of linguistic obtuseness or dishonesty with moral torpor or degeneracy, may be an indication that the satirist was "succumbing to the curse of Vienna—the city in which the experiment of replacing morality and politics by the life of the imagination was carried to the point of moral paralysis and political disintegration."[11] *Dichtung*—literature—meant to Kraus exclusively *Sprachgestaltung*—linguistic form. "Opinions,

10. Heinrich Fischer, Afterword to Karl Kraus, *Die Sprache* (Munich: Kösel, 1954), p. 441.
11. Stern, p. 83.

trends, *Weltanschauungen*," he wrote in 1921, "what matters first of all is only the sentence. . . . All my life I have cared about nothing but sentences, trusting that the truth about mankind, its wars and revolutions, its Jews and Christians will occur to them." Far from seeking linguistic expression for an idea, Kraus makes a thought come to him because he takes it by the word (or at its word, another possible meaning of "beim Wort"). "An aphorism need not be true, but it should overtake truth," he once wrote. "It must get beyond it *in einem Satz*." The last part of this aphorism defies translation; the German phrase means both "in one sentence" and "with one leap," and Kraus was fond of playing with—and even physically illustrating—this linguistic fortuitousness.

Despite the fact that Kraus raised language to an almost apocalyptic significance, however, he never developed a theory or philosophy of language, being essentially an unsystematic and anti-philosophical thinker. Yet the Vienna Circle of logical positivists was greatly interested in Kraus's relationship to language, and there are certain parallels between Kraus's thought and the ideas of Ludwig Wittgenstein, the foremost figure of that circle: their common insight, for example, into the fundamental connection between, or even identification of, ethics and esthetics. Wittgenstein learned from Kraus how to think in and through language, yet he thought *against* language—which for him, was an obstacle to thought that had to be painstakingly surmounted—whereas Kraus fought *for* language, mystically uncovering thought through it. Thus both Kraus and Wittgenstein strove to fashion, each from his own vision of language, a fortress capable of standing inviolate against the corruption of language and morals that they beheld all around them.

It is next to impossible, on a large scale, to convey in English an idea of Kraus's style, the most brilliant in modern German letters. The allusiveness of this style, its attention to verbal associations, and its artful plays upon words make reading Kraus in the original an intellectual delight. Kraus was not only a master of the art of punning, with a deep seriousness underlying his verbal wit, but also a skillful practitioner of various subtle stylistic devices based upon the spirit of German grammar and Kraus's enjoyment of what he called *Sprachlehre*.

The aphorism was a literary sub-genre that Kraus employed extensively. Many of his aphoristic sayings were distilled from a longer text that had originally appeared in prose or verse; in other cases an aphorism came, in time, to be lyrically expanded into an epigram, or was made to serve as the nucleus of a prose piece. The aphorisms that make up the present selection are drawn from the collection *Beim Wort genommen* (ed. Heinrich Fischer, 1955) which incorporates three smaller collections published by Kraus in his lifetime: *Sprüche und Widersprüche* (1909), *Pro domo et mundo* (1912), and *Nachts* (1918).

Both the choice and the translation of these aphorisms posed certain problems. Any selection from the work of any writer is bound to be subjective and necessarily reflects the taste and the judgment of one editor or anthologist. When translatability becomes the prime criterion for inclusion or non-inclusion, as must needs be the case with Karl Kraus, a selection cannot be fully representative of the writer's work as a whole. In this particular instance, it should be noted that many of the most brilliant and characteristic of Kraus's thousands of aphorisms, especially those dealing with language, imagination, the artistic process, and verbal creativity, have had to be excluded because of their essential untranslatability. In many cases the aphorist drew his inspiration from the inexhaustible reservoir of language, to use a Krausian locution, and these ideas remain inextricably tied to the German language and its genius. In other cases so many explanatory notes would have been needed to unravel the complexity and allusiveness of the original aphorisms that the thrust of Kraus's ideas would have been blunted or completely destroyed. As a result, what *can* be offered remains in many instances the *Meinungen* (opinions) that Kraus abhorred rather than the *Gedanken* (ideas) that he wished to convey. Yet a sufficiently rounded picture of Kraus the person and the artist may emerge to convince the reader that Kraus's aphorism about a linguistic work translated into another language being comparable to crossing a border without one's skin and putting on the local garb on the other side is itself a "half-truth."

One or two examples may serve to clarify both Kraus's imaginative response to language and the difficulties inherent in transferring this response to another language. The aphorism "Man lebt nicht einmal einmal" is rendered "You don't even live once"; the trite German saying "Man lebt nur einmal," which has an English equivalent in the (equally trite) hedonistic

"You only live once," has been turned around by Kraus. The English translation offered here seems to reflect a pessimistic *Weltanschauung*, a mere opinion. Yet Kraus has utilized the possibilities of the German language to give verbal play to an idea directly derived from this language: *einmal*, stressed on the first syllable and meaning "once," is preceded by *einmal*, stressed on the second syllable and meaning—in conjunction with *nicht*—"not even." As Edward Timms points out, to reproduce the syntactical uniqueness of German and still convey Kraus's thought (which is basically life-affirming), one would have to use the analogous (though not fully equivalent) resources of the English language, ending up with a version of Kraus's aphorism that would read something like this: "One's chances of living a happy life are not even even." Yet such a rendition would have no place in the present volume; it would be a *Nachdichtung*, a free and somewhat labored re-creation, rather than an *Übersetzung*, a translation.

Another case in point where an English rendition at best results in a compromise that, however ingenious, cannot do full justice to a devastatingly witty idea is Kraus's aphorism "Je grösser der Stiefel, desto grösser der Absatz." On the face of it, this is a shoemaker's truism: "The bigger the boot, the bigger the heel." But in colloquial German, *Stiefel* also means "blather" or "nonsense," and another meaning of *Absatz* is "sale." The translation in this book, "The bigger the bull, the bigger the bull market," still does not convey all the levels of meaning and the language-derived ideas in Kraus's aphorism, especially when one considers that yet another meaning of *Absatz* is "paragraph." (In view of Kraus's interminable paragraphs, the satirist's detractors might well use this aphorism against him.)

To sum up: the reader should not, on the basis of an isolated statement, attempt to pigeonhole Kraus in this or that category. Kraus was the most mercurial of thinkers; apparent inconsistencies and contradictions in his writings had for him no significance. Wrote the satirist himself: "He who expresses opinions must not let himself be caught in a contradiction. He who has ideas thinks amidst contradictions as well." As noted above, Kraus trusted in the power of his individual sentences to supply truths about the various masks and endeavors of humankind. If the selection of aphorisms that follows provides at least a glimpse into the workings of a fascinating mind, it will count itself a success.

H.Z.

BRANDEIS UNIVERSITY

Waltham, Massachusetts
November 1975

In the literary prism
Nothing more enlightens, nothing hooks
Ampler meaning than the aphorism,
Scoring better than a shelf of books.
Half a truth is ideal,
Three-quarters would be unreal.

ROY C. BATES

With my narrow horizon

I believe I can say this about myself, that I go along
with the development of Judaism up to the Exodus, but
that I don't participate in the dance around the Golden
Calf—and from that point on share only in those char-
acteristics which were also found in the defenders of
God and in the avengers of a people gone astray.

Honestly, they say, he lacks love (they say), love for
mankind. They must be awful pessimists who regard
the present collection as the best imaginable! Or awful
idiots who call someone a butterfly-hater who at the
thought of a dead admiral thinks there are too many
cabbage butterflies.

Am I to blame if hallucinations and visions are alive
and have names and permanent residences?

I hear noises which others don't hear and which disturb for me the music of the spheres, which others don't hear either.

I can imagine that an ugly woman who looks in the mirror is convinced that it is her mirror image, and not she, that is ugly. Thus society sees the mirror image of its meanness and is stupid enough to believe that I am the mean fellow.

Many share my views with me. But I don't share them with them.

It so often happened to me that someone who shared my opinion kept the larger share for himself that I am now forewarned and offer people only ideas.

An acquaintance of mine told me that reading one of my essays aloud gained him a wife. I count this among my greatest successes. How easily I could have been in this unfortunate situation myself.

When I want to go to sleep, I must first get a whole menagerie of voices to shut up. You wouldn't believe what a racket they make in my room.

My enemies have been looking for motives for ten years. I act this way because I didn't get the bread and butter—or even though I *did*. There is no doubt that bread and butter are involved; the only choice is between vindictiveness and ingratitude. That an action cannot spring from both motives at once gives my enemies a great deal of discomfort. But I would gladly admit to both if I could only escape the crushing question which well-meaning people direct at me: "Tell me, I beg of you, what have you got against Benedikt?"

From a torch something drops occasionally. A little lump of pitch.

In one ear and out the other: this would still make the head a transit station. What I hear has to go out the same ear.

I'd like to apply for a permit to run a hand-operated guillotine. But oh, that income tax!

I put my pen to the Austrian corpse because I persist in believing there's life in it.

What others offer as an objection often is my premise —for example, that my polemics attack someone's livelihood. Yet I have never attacked a person for his or her own sake, even if that person was named. If I were a journalist, I would be proud to censure a king. But since I tackle a crowd of carters, it is megalomaniacal if an individual feels offended. If I name names, this is done only because a name heightens the plastic effect of satire. After ten years of artistic work, my victims ought to be sufficiently trained to see that and stop lamenting at last.

I ask no one for a light. I don't want to be beholden to anyone—in life, love, or literature. And yet I smoke.

I have often been asked to be fair and view a matter from all sides. I did so, hoping that something might improve if I viewed all sides of it. But the result was the same. So I went back to viewing things only from one side, which saves me a lot of work and disappointment. For it is comforting to regard something as bad and to be able to use one's prejudice as an excuse.

I and my public understand each other very well: it does not hear what I say, and I don't say what it wants to hear.

The blind won't admit that I have eyes in my head, and the deaf say that I'm dumb.

If someone calls me vain and mean, I know that he trusts me and has something to confess to me.

What is my love? That I amalgamate the bad features of a woman into a good picture. And my hatred? That I see the bad features in the bad picture of a man.

I no longer have collaborators. I used to be envious of them. They repel those readers whom I want to lose myself.

My readers think that I write for the day because my writings are based on the day. So I shall have to wait until my writings are obsolete. Then they may acquire timeliness.

An understanding of my work is impeded by a knowledge of my material. People don't realize that what is there must first be invented, and that it is worth inventing. Nor do they see that a satirist for whom people exist as though he had invented them needs more strength than one who invents persons as though they existed.

How much material I would have if nothing happened!

I (with my narrow horizon) once neglected to read a newspaper page that contained these headlines: "The Secret Negotiations between Austria, France, and Italy in 1869," "The Reform Movement in Persia," "The Appointment of the Croatian Department Heads," "The Sublime Porte versus the Metropolitan of Monastir." After not reading this page I felt that my horizon was a bit widened.

At my desk at night, in an advanced state of intellectual enjoyment, the presence of a woman would disturb me more than the intervention of a Germanist in my bedroom.

In literary work I find enjoyment, and literary enjoyment becomes work for me. To enjoy the work of another mind, I must first take a critical attitude toward it—transform reading, that is, into work. For which reason I shall more easily and more gladly write a book than read one.

Often I prick my hand with my pen and know only then that I have experienced what is written.

When I read, it is not acted literature; but what I write is written acting.

What could be even more fascinating than the suspense as to what the place which I have so often imagined will look like? The suspense of how I restore my imagination after I have seen the place.

Word and substance—that is the only connection I have ever striven for in my life.

When someone is about to accost me, I hope till the last moment that the fear of being compromised will keep him from doing so. But people are intrepid.

If I return some people's greetings, I do so only to give them their greeting back.

I divide the people whom I don't greet into four groups. There are those whom I don't greet in order not to compromise myself. This is the simplest group. Next, there are those whom I don't greet in order not to compromise *them*. This requires a certain amount of attention. But then there are those whom I don't greet in order not to get into their bad books. They are even harder to deal with. And finally there are those whom I don't greet in order not to get into *my* bad books. This takes a particular amount of concentration. But I've had quite a bit of practice, and by my manner of not greeting people I manage to express each of those nuances in such a way that no injustice is done to anyone.

Why, he's the one who thought I've forgotten that I don't know him!

I am already so popular that someone who vilifies me becomes more popular than I am.

Nothing is more horrible than my self in the mirror of hysteria. Nothing is more vulgar than my style in the hands of another. To imitate me is to punish me.

I trim my opponents to fit my arrows.

I can irritate them all. But to soothe each individual exceeds my strength.

My attacks are so unpopular that only the rogues of the future will understand me.

Many desire to kill me, and many wish to spend an

hour chatting with me. The law protects me from the former.

What torture, this life in society! Often someone is obliging enough to offer me a light, and in order to oblige *him* I have to fish a cigarette out of my pocket.

"You do him an injustice. He agrees with you on everything." "Except with the fact that I regard him as an ass."

Life in Vienna is beautiful. All day long a flute plays on me.

One's need for loneliness is not satisfied if one sits at a table alone. There must be empty chairs as well. If the waiter takes away a chair on which no one is sitting, I feel a void and my sociability is aroused. I can't live without empty chairs.

I dreamt that I had died for my country. And right away a coffin-lid opener was there, holding out his hand for a tip.

"You are Herr Karl Kraus, aren't you?" asked a young man who was sharing my compartment on a train and who had overestimated my defenselessness. "No," I said, which meant that I admitted it. Because if I had been someone else, I would have started a conversation with that idiot.

Sorrento, August. For two weeks now I haven't heard a German word or understood an Italian one. This way one can manage to live with people; everything goes like clockwork and no irksome misunderstanding can arise.

Nationalism is the love which ties me to the blockheads of my country, to the insultors of my way of life, and to the desecrators of my language.

Nothing is more narrow-minded than chauvinism or race hatred. To me all men are equal: there are jack-asses everywhere, and I have the same contempt for all. No petty prejudices!

Oh no, I'm not a bellyacher. My hatred of Vienna is not love gone astray. It's just that I've discovered a completely new way of finding it unbearable.

I must be with people again. For this summer—among bees and dandelions—my misanthropy really got out of hand.

He who gladly does without the praise of the crowd will not miss the opportunity of becoming his own fan.

I take the liberty of conferring on myself all the blessings of a coterie.

Kokoschka has done a portrait of me. It could be that those who know me will not recognize me; but surely those who don't know me will recognize me.

I don't like to meddle in my private affairs.

My defects belong to me. This gives me the courage to express my good qualities as well.

My respect for the inconsiderable is assuming gigantic dimensions.

To me it still is a greater miracle when a fly flies than when a human being undertakes to do so.

I feed on scruples which I prepare for myself.

Drawing of Karl Kraus by Oskar Kokoschka, 1909/10

I eat greedily out of greed for non-eating.

When I have my hair cut, I worry that the barber might cut one of my thoughts.

I would have stage-fright if I had to speak with every one of the people before whom I speak.

I like to hold a monologue with women. But a dialogue with myself is more stimulating.

Many gentlemen to whom I have given walking papers have felt offended in their most feminine feelings.

Since the law prohibits the keeping of wild animals and I get no enjoyment from pets, I prefer to remain unmarried.

If I were sure that I should have to share immortality with certain people, I would prefer a separate oblivion.

Many things that I am experiencing I already remember.

X said disparagingly that nothing would remain of me but a few good jokes. That, at least, would be something, but unfortunately not even that will remain, for the few good jokes were stolen long ago—by X.

To those who have doubts about my health I will admit that I suffer from gout. But I won't let anyone deny that I can also feel a thunderstorm coming.

When the end of the world comes, I want to be living in retirement.

When the horse stepped up on the sidewalk the coachman said: "He's still young; he's gotta practice." "But not on me," I said. When the horse stepped up on the sidewalk the coachman said: "He don't see so good no more." Once in my life I would like to encounter a good horse!

I and life: The case was settled chivalrously. The opponents parted without having made up.

A man gets so little recognition he could turn into a megalomaniac.

When I take up my pen, nothing can happen to me. Fate, remember that.

Riddles out of solutions

In art the important thing is not that one takes eggs and fat, but that one has a fire and a pan.

Love and art do not embrace what is beautiful but what is made beautiful by this embrace.

If by day art is in the service of business, the evenings are devoted to the businessman's enjoyment of it. That is asking a lot of art, but art and the businessman make it work.

Science is spectral analysis. Art is light synthesis.

Oh, for this race with those interminable stimuli! And this perpetual long-distance run from stimulus to art! At the goal, panting—dragged back to the start, which feels reached.

Imagination has the right to feast in the shade of the tree that it turns into a forest.

To write a feuilleton is to curl locks on a bald head—but the public likes such curls better than a lion's mane of thought.

A plagiarist should be made to copy the author a hundred times.

To have talent, to be a talent: the two are always confused.

His way of pushing into the background was a general nuisance.

This author is so deep that it took me, the reader, a long time to get to his surface.

Something I cannot get over: that a whole line could be written by half a man. That a work could be built on the quicksand of a character.

In the theater one must sit in such a way that one sees the audience as a dark mass. Then it cannot bother one more than it does an actor. Nothing is more disturbing than being able to distinguish individuals in the crowd.

The opera: consistency of character and reality of events are qualities which need not be accompanied by music.

Once upon a time the actors were genuine and the decorations of cardboard; nowadays the decorations do not give rise to doubt—and the actors are of cardboard.

I do not trust the printing press when I deliver my written words to it. How a dramatist can rely on the mouth of an actor!

On the stage one must not confuse the nature of a personality with the naturalness of a person.

The art of an actress is sublimated sexuality. But off the stage the fire must be able to reconvert the steam into body.

One can discover an actress by letting her portray the most natural situation a woman can get herself into.

The new dramatic art: dilettantes without stage-fright.

The only art in which the public has a sound judgment is dramatic art. An individual spectator, especially a critic, talks nonsense, but all spectators together are right. With literature it is just the other way round.

That an author takes a bow is not humility but presumption. What does that paleface want on the stage afterwards? But before the performance he had even less business there—and paying him royalties is equivalent to cheating the actors.

An artist who makes concessions achieves no more than the traveler abroad who tries to make himself understood by speaking broken German.

Only he is an artist who can make a riddle out of a solution.

I saw a poet chase a butterfly in a meadow. He put his net on a bench where a boy sat reading a book. It's a misfortune that it is usually the other way round.

A philistine is habitually bored and looks for things that won't bore him. An artist finds things boring, but is never bored.

Nestroy's words ought to apply to an artist and an idea: "I have made a prisoner, and he won't let go of me."

Why should one artist grasp another? Does Mount Vesuvius appreciate Mount Etna? At most, a feminine relationship of jealous comparison might develop: Who spits better?

Artists have a right to be modest and a duty to be vain.

An artist should make concessions to the listener. That is why Bruckner dedicated one of his symphonies to the Good Lord.

Today's literature: prescriptions written by patients.

In the beginning was the review copy, and a man received it from the publisher. Then he wrote a review. Then he wrote a book which the publisher accepted and sent on to someone else as a review copy. The man who received it did likewise. This is how modern literature came into being.

Most critics write critiques which are by the authors they write critiques about. That would not be so bad, but then most authors write works which are by the critics who write critiques about them.

A poem is good until one knows by whom it is.

Most writers have no other quality than the reader: taste. But the latter has the better taste, because he does not write—and the best if he does not read.

Scholarship could make itself useful. A writer needs all its subjects to supply the raw material for his images, and often he lacks a term which he surmises but does not know. Looking it up is bothersome, boring, and overly informative. Therefore, while a writer is working, people ought to be sitting in the other rooms and come running on a signal when the writer has something to ask them. One ring for the historian, two for the economist, three for the handyman who has been to medical school, and perhaps four for the Talmudic scholar who also masters the jargon of philosophy. But none of them should be permitted to say more than what they are asked about, and they would have to leave immediately after answering because their proximity is not stimulating beyond the services they render. One could, of course, do without such aids altogether, and an artistic simile would retain its value even if an educational gap in its formulation might later bring censure from an expert. But it would be an opportunity to give the experts an occupation as useful as it is glorious and spare them subsequent annoyance.

Wanted: a suitable desert for a Fata Morgana.

My writings must be read twice if one is to get close to them. But I don't object to their being read three times. However, I prefer their not being read at all to their being read only once. I would not want to be responsible for the congestions of a blockhead who has no time. . . . One must read all writers twice—the good as well as the bad. The one kind will be recognized; the other, unmasked.

Let my style capture all the sounds of my time. This should make it an annoyance to my contemporaries. But later generations should hold it to their ears like a seashell in which there is the music of an ocean of mud.

To write a novel may be pure pleasure. To live a novel presents certain difficulties. As for reading a novel, I do my best to get out of it.

It is not easy to get a truly and constantly productive spirit to read. He is to a reader as a locomotive is to a tourist. Besides, one does not ask a tree how it likes the scenery.

Where shall I find the time to do all this non-reading?

Things might be better if German writers expended one-tenth of the care on their manuscripts which I expend in the printing of my writings. A friend who has often assisted me as a midwife was astonished to see how easy were my births and how arduous my childbed. The others are well off. They work at their desks and enjoy themselves in company. I enjoy myself at my desk and work in company. That is why I avoid company. At the most I could ask people which of the two words they like better. And this is something they don't know.

My request that my writings be read twice has aroused great indignation. Unjustly so. After all, I do not ask that they be read once.

People know my occasions personally. That's why they think my art is not that great.

Hate must make a person productive; otherwise one might as well love.

There are writers who can express in as little as twenty pages what I occasionally need as many as two for.

A good stylist should have narcissistic enjoyment as he works. He must be able to objectivize his work to such an extent that he catches himself feeling envious and has to jog his memory to find that he is himself the creator. In short, he must display that highest degree of objectivity which the world calls vanity.

My glosses need a commentary. Otherwise they are too easily understood.

My helplessness grows with the completion of what I have written. The closer I come to a word, the more it bleeds, like a corpse in the presence of the murderer. I do not spare myself this bier tribunal, and I cover the margin of a proofsheet—which may have been preceded by fifteen carefree ones—with marks that are like wounds. I always have at least two routes, and it would be best to take both and all of them. Eventually I shall probably bring myself to put down various versions of a sentence for the benefit of the reader, who will thus be forced to read a sentence several times, and to get very far away from those who only snatch at opinions. Until then I shall always have to leave the responsibility for the best of all good routes to the person I am consulting. His mechanical decision would suffice me, but since I could help him get out of a similar situation much better than he could help me, I don't make things that easy for us and plunge him so deep into the abyss of my doubts that I gain assurance from his situation, save him, and thus save myself as well.

Sound opinions are valueless. What matters is who holds them.

He who expresses opinions must not let himself be caught in a contradiction. He who has ideas thinks amidst contradictions as well.

It is better not to express what one means than to express what one does not mean.

In case of doubt, decide in favor of what is correct.

An idea's birth is legitimate only if one has the feeling that one is catching oneself plagiarizing oneself.

An idea is a love child. An opinion is recognized by bourgeois society.

Opinions are contagious; the idea is a miasma.

The real truths are those that can be invented.

A *Weltanschauung* is a good horse. But there is a difference between a fine equestrian and a horse dealer.

Sentimental irony is a dog that bays at the moon while pissing on graves.

I have a shattering bit of news for the esthetes: Old Vienna was new once.

If you wish to form a clear judgment on your friends, consult your dreams.

A slapstick comedian threw a toothpick behind the stage. There was a crash. Then he threw a pin backstage. There was a crash. Then he threw a piece of paper backstage. Again there was a crash. Then he picked up a feather, raised his arm—and again there was a crash. But he hadn't thrown it down yet. He made a gesture expressive of his pleasure at having fooled causality. It is the nature of this humor that the echo of human affairs is stronger than their call, and that the best way to prove to the echo that it is forward is not to answer it with a call.

One shouldn't learn more than what one absolutely needs against life.

What is the Ninth Symphony compared to a pop tune played by a hurdy-gurdy and a memory!

Satire chooses and knows no objects. It arises by fleeing from them and their forcing themselves upon it.

A man who feels offended by a satire behaves like the random partner for a night who comes around the next day to claim his personality. Another example has long since taken his place, and at the beginning of another oblivion that man appears with his memories and gets jealous. He is capable of compromising the woman.

One shouldn't always name names. What should be said is not that someone has done it, but that it was possible to do it.

Satires which the censor understands are rightly prohibited.

Through my satire I make little people so big that afterwards they are worthy objects of my satire and no one can reproach me any longer.

If a name is used for satirical effect, people object and say that the man is not to blame for his name. But neither is he to be blamed for his lack of talent, and yet I am inclined to believe that he must be castigated for the latter. Now it may be argued that a genius could bear the same name. But that would not be true, or rather, the name would then not be laughable. On the other hand, in a satirical mood one could find fault with the name Goethe if an oaf bore it. Just as everything about great men is great, everything about the ridiculous is laughable; and if a name opens up a source of humor, the bearer is to blame. He is justly named thus, and if in despair he takes refuge in a pseudonym, ridicule will manage to hit him there as well.

Language is the only chimera whose illusory power is endless, the inexhaustability which keeps life from being impoverished. Let men learn to serve language.

Let language be the divining rod that finds sources of thought.

Why do people treat literature so insolently? Because they know the language. They would take the same liberties with the other arts if singing to one another, smearing one another with paint, or throwing plaster at one another were means of communication. The unfortunate thing is that verbal art works with a material that the rabble handles every day. That is why literature is beyond help. The farther it removes itself from comprehensibility, the more importunately do people claim their material. The best thing would be to keep literature secret from the people until there is a law that prohibits people from using language, permitting them to use only sign language in urgent cases. But by the time such a law comes into being, they will probably have learned to answer the aria "How's business?" with a still life.

"He masters the German language"—that is true of a salesman. An artist is a servant of the word.

Language is the mother of thought, not its handmaiden.

The most incomprehensible talk comes from people who have no other use for language than to make themselves understood.

Language is the mother of thought? Thought is not to the credit of the thinker? Oh, but it is; the thinker must impregnate language.

Heinrich Heine so loosened the corsets of the German language that today every little salesman can fondle her breasts.

If one says of a German writer that the French were his teachers, it is the highest praise only if it is not true.

Heine was a Moses who struck the rock of the German language with his rod. But speed is not magic. The water did not flow from the rock; rather, he had brought it along in his other hand—and it was really *eau de Cologne*.

A linguistic work translated into another language is like someone going across the border without his skin and donning the local garb on the other side.

A pun, though despicable in itself, can be the noblest vehicle of an artistic intention by serving as the abbreviation of a witty view. It can be a social criticism in the form of an epigram.

Someone who can write aphorisms should not fritter away his time writing essays.

One cannot dictate an aphorism to a typist. It would take too long.

If there is a misprint in a sentence and it still makes sense, that sentence was not an idea.

One can translate an editorial but not a poem. For one can go across the border naked but not without one's skin; for, unlike clothes, one cannot get a new skin.

An aphorism never coincides with the truth: it is either a half-truth or one-and-a-half truths.

The closer the look one takes at a word, the greater the distance from which it looks back.

I have decided many a stylistic problem first by my head, then by heads or tails.

When I don't make any progress, it is because I have bumped into the wall of language. Then I draw back with a bloody head. And would like to go on.

People don't understand German. But I can't tell them things in journalese.

A poet's language, a woman's love—it it always that which happens for the first time.

I master only the language of others. Mine does with me what it wants.

You'd be surprised how hard it can often be to translate an action into an idea.

I have drawn from the well of language many a thought which I do not have and which I could not put into words.

All that Adolf Loos and I did—he literally, I linguistically—was to show that there is a difference between an urn and a chamberpot, and that in this difference there is leeway for culture.* But the others, the "positive ones," are divided into those who use the urn as a chamberpot and those who use the chamberpot as an urn.

My language is the common prostitute that I turn into a virgin.

*The architect Loos (1870–1933), a friend of Kraus, was a pioneer in utilitarian architecture and a foe of useless ornamentation.—Ed.

In hollow heads

Why didn't Eternity have this deformed age aborted?
Its birthmark is the stamp of a newspaper, its meconi-
um is printer's ink, and in its veins flows ink.

There are people among us still who look as though
they've just come from Christ's crucifixion, and there
are others who seem to be asking, What did he say?
Yet others exist who write it all down under the title
"The Events on Golgotha."

The Finns say: Without us there'd be no ham!
The journalists say: Without us there'd be no culture!
The maggots say: Without us there'd be no corpses!

It would be possible to get along with the perfect feuilletonists if they did not have their eye on immortality. They know how to present the values of others and have at their fingertips everything that they don't have in their heads, frequently showing good taste. If you want a window decorated, you don't call in a lyric poet. He might be able to do the work, but he doesn't. It's a window decorator's job, and this is what gives him a social status which the poet justly envies him. A window decorator can come to the attention of posterity too—but only if the poet writes a poem about him.

The noun is the head, the verb is the foot, the adjective is the hands. Journalists write with their hands.

Newspapers have roughly the same relationship to life as fortune tellers to metaphysics.

Journalism only *seems* to be serving the present. In reality it destroys the intellectual receptivity of posterity.

A journalist is stimulated by a deadline. He writes worse when he has time.

It is the mission of the press to disseminate intellect and at the same time destroy receptivity to it.

The making of a journalist: no ideas and the ability to express them.

Journalists write because they have nothing to say, and have something to say because they write.

What is a historian? Someone who doesn't write well enough to work on a daily.

A historian is often only a journalist facing backwards.

A historian is not always a prophet facing backwards, but a journalist is always someone who afterwards knew everything beforehand.

There is a shortage of clerks. Everyone is going into journalism.

It is a mystery to me how a theologian can be praised for having brought himself to disbelieve dogmas. I've always thought that those who have brought themselves to *believe* in dogmas merit the true recognition owing a heroic deed.

I knew a man who carried his education in his vest pocket because there was more room there than in his head.

Education is what most people receive, many pass on, and few have.

I can say with pride that I have spent days and nights not reading anything, and that with unflagging energy I use every free moment to acquire gradually an encyclopedic lack of education.

A comprehensive education is a well-stocked pharmacy: but we have no assurance that potassium cyanide will not be administered for a head cold.

A school without grades must have been concocted by someone who was drunk on non-alcoholic wine.

A bibliophile has approximately the same relationship to literature as a philatelist to geography.

I had a terrible vision: I saw an encyclopedia walk up to a polymath and open him up.

What the teachers digest, the pupils eat.

A pundit once boasted that he moved his library with straps. These are not cheap, he said, but they last a lifetime. He used three hundred straps. That's quite a lot. And yet it's a handy measure. Look, the man has a three-hundred-strap education! He thinks by the strap. He isn't even a freethinker. Oh yes, he needs three hundred straps not to go under.

In a hollow head there is much room for knowledge.

The trading mentality is said to have evolved in the confines of the ghetto streets. In freedom they indulge in psychology. . . . What miracles a combination of trading mentality and psychology can produce we see every day.

In a well-run mental household there ought to be a thorough cleaning at the threshold of consciousness a few times a year.

Analysis is the tendency of a schnorrer to explain how riches come into being. Invariably that which he does not possess has been acquired by deceit. The other fellow just has it; but fortunately the analyst is in the know.

One of the most widespread diseases is diagnosis.

Psychoanalysis is that mental illness for which it regards itself as therapy.

The difference between psychiatrists and other mentally disturbed people is something like the relationship between concave and convex madness.

An analyst turns man into dust.

Most people are sick. But only few know that this is something they can be proud of. These are the psychoanalysts.

So-called psychoanalysis is the occupation of lustful rationalists who trace everything in the world to sexual causes—with the exception of their occupation.

They pick our dreams as if they were our pockets.

The child of psychoanalytic parents withers early. As an infant such a child has to admit that he has voluptuous feelings when he moves his bowels. Later he is asked what the defecation of a horse he has watched on the way to school makes him think of. Such a child is lucky if he grows up to be a young man who is able to confess that he raped his mother in a dream.

The new psychiatrists say that everything and anything can be traced back to sexual causes. Their method, for example, could be explained as the eroticism of father confessors.

Psychoanalysts are father confessors who like to listen to the sins of the fathers as well.

The highest position of trust: father confessor for sins not committed.

According to the latest research, the subconscious seems to be a sort of ghetto of ideas. Many are now homesick.

Psychology is a bus that accompanies an airplane.

Psychoanalysis: a rabbit that was swallowed by a boa constrictor just wanted to see what it was like in there.

Disclosure at the end of a psychoanalytic cure: "Well, you can't be cured. You are sick!"

Psychology is as useless as directions for using poison.

One cleans someone else's threshold of consciousness only if one's own home is dirty.

Your conscious probably hasn't much use for my unconscious. But I have implicit faith in my unconscious; it will be able to cope with your conscious.

If something is stolen from you, don't go to the police. They're not interested. Don't go to a psychologist either, because he's interested in only one thing: that it was really *you* who did the stealing.

They have the press, they have the stock exchange, and now they also have the subconscious!

In this war we are dealing . . .

Yes, it is a chlorious war.

A sorcerer's apprentice seems to have utilized the absence of his master. But now there is blood instead of water.

How is the world ruled and led to war? Diplomats lie to journalists and believe these lies when they see them in print.

War is, at first, the hope that one will be better off; next, the expectation that the other fellow will be worse off; then, the satisfaction that he isn't any better off; and, finally, the surprise at everyone's being worse off.

It makes sense to die for a fatherland in which one cannot live. But I, as a patriot, would prefer suicide to a
defeat.

What mythological confusion is this? Since when has
Mars been the god of commerce and Mercury the god
of war?

Someone said: "This command will be carried out
promptly." What he meant to say was: "This battle
will be supplied promptly."

One ought to acknowledge the significance for mankind of the simultaneous invention of gunpowder and
printer's ink.

Among some nations, the aptitude for reading war com-
muniqués is by now probably a substitute for the
fitness to fight.

At the door of a German military office I saw a poster on which these words stood out: "Free Soldiers!" But it meant that civilians were wanted to do clerical work so as to enable the soldiers working there to go to the front.

Mankind is supposed to regain its health in war? If it does not infect war!

Diplomacy is a game of chess in which the nations are checkmated.

A *franc-tireur* is a civilian who intentionally attacks an armed man. A flier is an armed man who accidentally kills a civilian.

"How can you sympathize so with the English? You don't even know English." "No, but I know German!"

The enemy's demand that the German artillery surrender is madness. Only a demand for the surrender of the German *Weltanschauung* would be logical, and such a demand is unfulfillable.

If need be, bowling-club humor will even throw bombs with jokes.

What can be decided by a world war? No more than that Christianity was too weak to prevent it.

"The end is not yet in sight." "Oh, but it is!"

"Father, bread!" "Children, Russia is starving!"

What good are flame throwers to us when we are runing out of matches?

If someone had told the devil (to whom war has always been pure pleasure) that one day there would be people with an unfeigned commercial interest in the continuation of the war—the profits from which even helped them to attain social standing—why, the devil would have directed that person to go tell it to the marines. But later, after he had verified this fact, hell would have glowed with shame and he would have been forced to the realization that all his life he had been but a poor devil!

Sacrificing cotton to save one's life I can understand. But the other way round?

If bookkeepers wage war, they should also calculate the chances.

I can't help thinking that there is a causal connection between our superior artillery on the one hand and the high price of fruit and the conditions on the streetcar, with all that human misery muddling along and seeing it through, on the other.

Many of those who were full of enthusiasm on 1 August 1914 and also had butter hoped there would be even more butter on 1 August 1917. They can still remember the enthusiasm.

"To capture the world market"—because merchants spoke thus, warriors had to act thus. Since then there have been captures, though not of the world market.

When the word "peace" was uttered for the first time, there was panic at the stock exchange. They screamed in pain: "We've been earning! Leave us the war! We've earned the war!"

Paternoster is a kind of elevator. Bethlehem is a place in America where the biggest munitions factory is located.

"In this war we are dealing. . . ." "Yessiree, in this war we are dealing!"

If one speaks of a "war of quantities," one seems to be acknowledging the necessity of war as such, because it may at least solve the problem of overpopulation. But could this noble purpose not be attained more painlessly by legalizing abortion? "The prevailing morality," I can hear this morality say, "would never approve of this!" I didn't think it would, because the prevailing morality only approves of women having children so that these can be torn to bits by bombs!

That claim to a place in the sun is well known. But it is less well-known that the sun will have set before the place has been attained.

No, there won't be any scar left on the soul. The bullet will have gone in mankind's one ear and out the other.

Children play soldier. That makes sense. But why do soldiers play children?

The real end of the world is the destruction of the spirit; the other kind depends on the insignificant attempt to see whether after such a destruction the world can go on.

"Are you moved by the many who are dying now?"
"I weep for the survivors, and there are more of those."

What I believe: That if this war does not kill off the good people, it may produce a moral island for the good who were good even without it. But that it will transform the entire surrounding world into one vast hinterland of deceit, infirmity, and the most inhuman blasphemy, in that evil, transcending the war and continuing to be activated by it, will grow fat behind ideals used as a front and feed on its victims. That in this war, the war of today, civilization does not renew itself but saves itself from the hangman only by committing suicide. That the war has been more than sin: lies, daily lies from which printer's ink flowed like blood, one feeding on the other, diverging, a delta to the great water of madness. That this war of today is nothing but an eruption of peace and that it cannot be ended by peace but by the war of the universe against this mad-dog planet! That human victims had to fall unprece-dentedly—not deplorable because someone else's will drove them to the slaughter, but tragic because they had to atone for an unknown guilt. That someone who feels the unexampled injustice which even the most wicked of worlds does to itself as personal torture has only one last moral task left: mercilessly to sleep away this anxious waiting period until he is released by the Word or by the impatience of God.

"You, too, are an optimist who believes and hopes that the world is going to ruin."

No, it is proceeding only like my nightmare; and when I wake up, it will be all over.

Vae victoribus!

Not for women but against men

A fine world in which man reproaches woman with fulfilling his heart's desire!

Oberons will never understand that Titania can caress an ass, too, because owing to their lesser sexuality they would not be capable of caressing a she-ass. But in love they themselves become asses.

The Christian zoo: A tamed lioness sits in a cage. Many lions stand outside and look in with interest. Their curiosity is increased by the obstacle of the bars. Finally they break them. The attendants wring their hands and flee.

Insights into erotic life belong to art, not to education. But sometimes these have to be spelled out for the illiterates. And it is mainly a matter of convincing the illiterates, for they are the ones who write the penal code.

It is high time for children to enlighten their parents about the secrets of sex.

Sexual enlightenment is that hard-hearted process which for hygienic reasons forbids young people to satisfy their curiosity themselves.

Chastity always takes its toll. In some it produces pimples; in others, sex laws.

If children had been told they could not blow their noses, this alone would make adults blush.

There is a pedagogy which at Eastertime decides to break it gently to young people just what hangs from the Christmas tree in that mysterious room.

Sex education is legitimate in that girls cannot be taught soon enough how children don't come into the world.

A man's jealousy is a social institution; a woman's prostitution is an instinct.

The moral order has done justice to the mysterious abilities of women to be prostituted and to prostitute by creating two monogamous institutions: the mistress and the pimp.

Christianity has enriched the erotic meal with the appetizer of curiosity and spoiled it with the dessert of remorse.

Love between the sexes is a sin in theology, a forbidden understanding in jurisprudence, a mechanical insult in medicine—and philosophy doesn't bother with that sort of thing at all.

Erotic pleasure is an obstacle course.

Ballerinas have their sexuality in their legs, tenors in their larynxes. That is why women are mistaken about tenors and men about ballerinas.

A man's eroticism is a woman's sexuality.

The immorality of men triumphs over the amorality of women.

The woman takes one for all, the man all for one.

I am not for women but against men.

They treat women like a refreshing potion, refusing to admit that a woman may be thirsty.

A "seducer" who boasts of initiating women into the mystery of love is like a stranger who arrives at a railroad station and offers to show the sights to a tourist guide.

Moral responsibility is what is lacking in a man when he demands it of a woman.

A connoisseur of women who falls in love is like a doctor who picks up an infection at a sickbed. An occupational hazard.

Greek thinkers did not disdain whores. Germanic salesmen cannot live without ladies.

It is not the custom to marry a woman who has previously had an affair. But it is the custom to have an affair with a woman who has previously got married.

How nice when a girl forgets her good upbringing!

It is regarded as normal to consecrate virginity in general and to lust for its destruction in particular.

Virginity is the ideal of those who want to deflower.

I once knew a continent Don Giovanni whose Leporello wasn't even capable of compiling a list of unapproachable women.

Blushing, palpitations, a bad conscience—this is what you get if you haven't sinned.

She entered into matrimony with a lie. She was a virgin and failed to tell him!

There is no more unfortunate creature under the sun than a fetishist who yearns for a woman's shoe and has to settle for the whole woman.

To divide people into sadists and masochists is almost as foolish as dividing them into eaters and digesters. In all cases one must disregard abnormalities; after all, there are people who are better at digesting than they are at eating, and vice versa. As regards masochism and sadism, it is safe to say that a healthy person displays both perversities. The only ugly thing in each case is the word. The one derived from the novelist [Leopold von Sacher-Masoch] is particularly degrading, and it is hard not to let one's taste for things be spoiled by the designation. Nevertheless, a man with an artistic imagination will manage to let an authentic woman turn him into a masochist and an inauthentic one into a sadist. One knocks the latter's educated unnaturalness out of her until the woman is revealed. If she already is a woman, the only thing left to do is adore her.

A healthy man is content with a woman. An erotic man is content with a stocking to get to a woman. A sick man is content with the stocking.

True jealousy wants not only fidelity, but the proof of fidelity as an imaginable situation. A jealous man is not content with his beloved not being unfaithful. Precisely that which she is not doing does not leave him in peace. But since there is no proving what is not done and the jealous man insists on proof, he ends up settling for proof of unfaithfulness.

Jealousy is a dog's bark which attracts thieves.

The triumph of morality: A thief who has broken into a bedroom claims his sense of shame has been outraged, and by threatening the occupants with exposure of an immoral act he blackmails them into not bringing charges for burglary.

What are all the orgies of Bacchus when compared to the intoxication of someone who completely surrenders to continence!

Nothing is more unfathomable than a woman's superficiality.

A woman must look so smart that her dumbness comes as a pleasant surprise.

Those women are best with whom one speaks least.

Hysteria is the curdled milk of motherhood.

Charitable women constitute a distinct and particularly dangerous form of sublimated sexuality: samaritiasis.

Circumscription: "He completely fills my ears with his voice," she said of a singer.

She said to herself: Sleep with him, okay—but no intimacies!

She had so much modesty that she blushed when caught not sinning.

The extraordinary ability of a woman to forget is not the same as the talent of a lady not to be able to remember.

Many women would like to dream with men without sleeping with them. Someone should point out to them that this is utterly impossible.

A lady does shine like the sun, but one must not confuse her with the sun, for the sun associates with so many people during the day, while a lady was created by God to warm a single bank director, something with which she has her hands full, so that she desires nothing else, because she knows that she will thrive until she gets cold and the bank director feels a desire to go to the sun, which associates with so many during the day, amen.

Cosmetics is the science of a woman's cosmos.

Better to excuse an ugly foot than an ugly stocking.

A woman who cannot be ugly is not beautiful.

Her face: a mediocre ensemble in which the nose stands out.

The eyes of a woman should mirror my thoughts, not hers.

She only lacked a flaw to be perfect.

How unreliable is the woman caught being faithful!
Today she is faithful to you, tomorrow to another.

After a woman has been away for a long time, one must
celebrate a festival of non-recognition with her.

A woman who uses vitriol is capable of reaching for
ink.

A woman should not even be of *my* opinion, let alone
hers.

A woman is, occasionally, quite a serviceable substitute
for masturbation. It takes an abundance of imagination, to be sure.

It is not true that one cannot live without a woman. It
is simply that one cannot have lived without one.

Many things that are tasteless at table are spicy in bed —and vice versa. The reason most liaisons are so unhappy is that this distinction between bed and table is never made.

Two people did not get married. Since then they have been living in mutual widowhood.

The conjugal bedroom is the coexistence of brutality and martyrdom.

He forced her to do her bidding.

The slave! She does with him just as he pleases.

Women are demanding the franchise, both the active and the passive kind.* Does this mean that they are to have the right to choose any man and should no longer be blamed for letting themselves be chosen by any man? Heaven forbid. They mean it politically. Men have put such desperate thoughts into their heads. Now men will have no other choice but to demand of the government that they be allowed to menstruate at last.

As long as there is a women's rights movement, men should at least regard themselves as duty-bound to discontinue chivalry. Nowadays one can't even take a chance and offer a woman a seat on the streetcar, for one can never be sure that one won't be insulting her and abridging her right to an equal share of the inconveniences of life. On the other hand, one ought to get into the habit of being chivalrous and accommodating toward the feminists in every way.

*Kraus plays with the word *Wahlrecht*, which can mean the right to choose and the right to vote, or alternately the right to vote and the right to run for office.—Ed.

"Women's rights" are men's duties.

A beggar was handed a jail sentence because he had sat on a bench "looking sad." In the present order of things, men are suspect who look sad as are women who look cheerful. Anyway, society prefers beggars to ladies of the evening, because the latter are dishonest cripples who derive profit from the physical defect of beauty.

Society needs women of bad character. Those who have no character are a dubious element.

Women at least have elegant dresses. But what can men use to cover their emptiness?

A woman whose sexuality is unending and a man who constantly has ideas: two ideals of humanity which mankind regards as pathological.

At some time in the world there must have been an immaculate conception of voluptuousness!

To love, to be deceived, to be jealous—that's easy enough. The other way is less comfortable: To be jealous, to be deceived, and to love!

Lord, forgive them . . .

Humanity and bestiality: when will the former finally be uttered with the flavor of hate and the latter with the flavor of love? Does a lion tear his fellow lion to pieces?

With most people I don't get as far as the soul, but I already have my doubts on the matter of the intestines. For I cannot believe that this wonderful mechanism was created to put a councillor of commerce together; and only an autopsy can convince me that a usurer has a spleen.

The superman is a premature ideal, one that presupposes man.

When there were no human rights, the exceptional individual had them. That was inhuman. Then equality was created by taking the human rights away from the exceptional individual.

All the talk and actions of the so-called responsible men of today would not have been possible in the nurseries of earlier centuries. In today's nurseries, at least, the argument of the rod cuts some ice. But human rights are the destructible toy of the grown-ups which they want to step on and therefore won't give up. If whipping were allowed, people would whip far less often than they now feel inclined to do. What does progress consist in? Has the desire for whipping been abolished? No, only the whip itself. In the days of serfdom the fear of being whipped was the counterpoise to the pleasure of whipping. Today there is no such counterpoise, but whipping does have a spur in the progressive pride with which the stupid proclaim their human rights. That's some freedom, the freedom from being whipped!

When someone has behaved like an animal, he says: "I'm only human!" But when he is treated like an animal, he says: "I'm human, too!"

A gourmet once told me that he preferred the scum of the earth to the cream of society.

The time is coming when the Golden Fleece will be furnished by the Golden Calf.

"A cigar," said the altruist, "a *cigar*, my good man, I cannot give you. But any time you need a *light*, just come round; mine is always lit."

If the earth had any idea of how afraid the comet is of contact with it!

The devil is an optimist if he thinks he can make people meaner.

The world is a prison in which solitary confinement is preferable.

There is no doubt that a dog is loyal. But does that mean we should emulate him? After all, he is loyal to people, not to other dogs.

Solitude would be an ideal state if one were able to pick the people one avoids.

Curses on the law! Most of my fellow men are the sad consequences of neglected abortions.

What do people have against convicts? Is living together in the pen of freedom, where young people engage in mutual psychology, any more beautiful?

Squeeze human nature into the straitjacket of criminal justice and crime will appear!

Penalties serve to deter those who are not inclined to commit any crimes.

Nowadays the thief cannot be distinguished from his victim. Neither has any valuable objects on him.

Medicine: "Your money and your life!"

Mankind became hysterical in the Middle Ages because it poorly repressed the sexual impressions of its Greek boyhood.

The Judas kiss which Christian civilization gave to the human spirit was the last sexual act it permitted.

When the tenants discovered that their landlady was a panderer they had it in mind to give her notice. But they remained in the house when the landlady informed them that she had changed her occupation—and was now only a usurer.

Humanity is the washerwoman of society that wrings out its dirty laundry in tears.

The pimp is the executive organ of immorality. The executive organ of morality is the blackmailer.

Scandal begins when the police put a stop to it.

In the struggle between nature and morality, perversity can be a trophy or a wound, depending on whether nature has taken it or morality has inflicted it.

Anesthesia: wounds without pain. Neurasthenia: pain without wounds.

Perhaps things would be better if people were given muzzles and dogs laws, if people were led around on leashes and dogs on religion. Rabies might then decrease in the same measure as politics.

Democracy means the permission to be everyone's slave.

Social reform is the desperate decision to remove corns from a person suffering from cancer.

Democracy divides people into workers and loafers. It makes no provision for those who have no time to work.

The secret of the demagogue is to appear as dumb as his audience so that these people can believe themselves as smart as he.

Parliamentarianism means putting political prostitution in barracks.

Morality is the tendency to pour out the baby with the bath water.

Family life is an encroachment on private life.

Who is going to cast out an error to which he has given birth and replace it with an adopted truth?

Morality is a burglar's tool whose merit lies in never being left behind at the scene of the crime.

Since the day man first tried to conquer space, the earth has been mobilizing.

Pangs of conscience are the sadistic stirrings of Christianity.

There are people who can never forgive a beggar for their not having given him anything.

Religion, morality, and patriotism are feelings that are manifested only when they are outraged.

They judge lest they be judged.

The ugliness of our time has retroactive force.

"Yesterday I was in Melk—such awful weather," someone suddenly says to me on the train. "They say that
Imperial Councillor Eder is dead," the man at the next
table suddenly says to me. "He's become a big man,"
someone suddenly says to me in a different tone of
voice on the streetcar, pointing as he does so to a man
who has just got off and whom he evidently is proud
to know. Thus, without having asked for it, I find out
what goes on inside my contemporaries. It isn't enough
for them that I see their outward ugliness. In the five
minutes we walk down the road of life together I'm
supposed to be informed about what stirs them, pleases
them, disappoints them. . . . This, and only this, is the
substance of our civilization: the speed with which
stupidity sucks us into its vortex. We too might be
stirred, pleased, or disappointed about something, but
whoosh! we are willy-nilly in Melk, at Eder's coffin, in

the career of the big man. People like us would never manage to affect our fellow men in a similar way. I pause because the sunset is blood-red as never before —and someone asks me for a light. I am in pursuit of an idea which has just turned the corner—and someone behind me cries "Ta–xi!" As long as a wine-garden owner and a shoemaker remained posters, life would be bearable. Fine, we'll commit their faces to memory. But suddenly they stand before us in the flesh, put their hands on our shoulders—and we break down like Don Giovanni when the Commendatore's statue comes to life.

There is a cultural taste which tries very hard to get rid of the lice in a fur coat. There is another which tolerates the lice and thinks the coat can be worn with them in it. And finally there is a taste which regards the lice as the most important thing about the coat and consequently places the coat at the lice's disposal.

An excellent pianist; but his playing must drown out the belching of good society after dinner.

Many talents preserve their precociousness right into old age.

A good writer does not receive anywhere near the number of poison-pen letters that is commonly assumed. Among a hundred jackasses there are not ten who will admit to being jackasses, and at most one who will put it in writing.

A snob is unreliable. The work he praises might just be good.

I knew a hero who reminded one of Siegfried with his thick skin, and of Achilles with the condition of his heel.

The Jews live in an inbreeding of humor. When among themselves it is quite all right for them to poke fun at one another. But woe if they should separate!

A storyteller differs from a politician only in that he has time. What both have in common is that the time has them.

Contemporaries live from second hand to mouth.

If a windbag hasn't had an audience all day, he gets hoarse.

Barbershop conversations are irrefutable proof that heads exist for the sake of hair.

When a potentate is to be honored, the schools are closed, work ceases, and traffic stops.

It is the height of ingratitude if a sausage calls a pig a pig.

A father's pride, laid on thick, has always made me wish that the fellow had at least experienced some pain during procreation.

People's children run around like puns that were not suppressed. They are the unfruitful jokes of the un-fruitful, a burden to their progenitors.

Children of today laugh at fathers who tell them about dragons. It is necessary to make fear a required subject; otherwise children will never learn it.

Ingratitude is often disproportionate to the benefaction received.

Not greeting people isn't enough. One also doesn't greet people one doesn't know.

When animals yawn, they have human faces.

Gratitude is commonly understood to be the willingness to put on ointment for the rest of one's life because one once suffered from lice.

Restaurants are opportunities for innkeepers to greet, guests to order, and waiters to eat.

The most scurrilous form in which human dignity displays itself: the angry face of a waiter when one has banged on the table after calling him in vain.

The whistle-stops are very proud of the fact that the express trains have to pass them by.

Plenty of horse traders now pin their hopes on Pegasus.

Experiences are savings which a miser puts aside. Wisdom is an inheritance which a wastrel cannot exhaust.

Truth is a clumsy servant that breaks the dishes while washing them.

The bigger the bull, the bigger the bull market.

Never have I grasped the meaning of the phrase "to strain at a gnat and swallow a camel" better than in Italy, where loving innkeepers spread a mosquito net over our beds.

A white lie is always pardonable. But he who tells the truth without compulsion merits no leniency.

The unattractive thing about chauvinism is not so much the aversion to other nations, but the love of one's own.

Prussia: freedom of movement with a muzzle. Austria: an isolation cell in which screaming is allowed.

The streets of Vienna are paved with culture, the streets of other cities with asphalt.

It's not that far to Egypt. But to get to South Station!

Through her political scandals Austria has managed to draw the big world's attention to herself—and at last is no longer confused with Australia.

Progress celebrates Pyrrhic victories over nature.

Progress makes purses out of human skin.

Technology is a servant who makes so much noise cleaning up in the next room that his master cannot make music.

The development of technology will leave only one problem: the infirmity of human nature.

He died, bitten by the Aesculapian serpent.

Life is an effort that deserves a better cause.

A weak man has doubts before a decision; a strong man has them afterwards.

Ask your neighbor only about things you know better yourself. Then his advice could prove valuable.

Keep your passions in check, but beware of giving your reason free rein.

You don't even live once.

To be human is erroneous.

Lord, forgive them, for they know what they do!

Selected Bibliography

The standard Kraus bibliography is Otto Kerry, *Karl-Kraus-Bibliographie*, Munich: Kösel-Verlag, 1970. The present listing is limited to writings on Kraus which have appeared in English during the past three decades. With one or two exceptions, dissertations and book reviews are not included.

BODINE, JAY F.   "Karl Kraus's Conception of Language." *Modern Austrian Literature* 8, nos. 1 & 2 (1975): 268–309.

DAVIAU, DONALD G.   "The Heritage of Karl Kraus." *Books Abroad* 38 (1964): 248–256.

———. "Language and Morality in Karl Kraus's *Die letzten Tage der Menschheit*." *Modern Language Quarterly* 22 (1961): 46–54.

ENGELMANN, PAUL.   "Kraus, Loos, and Wittgenstein." In *Letters from Ludwig Wittgenstein, With a Memoir*, pp. 122–132. Oxford: Basil Blackwell, 1967.

FIELD, FRANK.   *The Last Days of Mankind: Karl Kraus and His Vienna*. New York: St. Martin's Press; London: Macmillan & Co., 1967.

FISCHER, HEINRICH.   "The Other Austria and Karl Kraus." In *In Tyrannos: Four Centuries of Struggle against Tyranny in Germany*, edited by H. J. Rehfisch, pp. 309–328. London: Lindsay Drummond, 1944.

GRIMSTAD, KARI. "Karl Kraus and the Problem of Illusion and Reality in Drama and the Theater." *Modern Austrian Literature* 8, nos. 1 & 2 (1975): 48–60.

HANSER, RICHARD. "Karl Kraus: A Torchbearer for His Time." *American-German Review* 34 (1968): 24–27.

HELLER, ERICH. "Karl Kraus: The Last Days of Mankind." In *The Disinherited Mind*, pp. 235–256. New York: Farrar, Straus & Cudahy, 1957.

————. "Dark Laughter." *New York Review of Books*, 3 May 1973, pp. 21–25.

IGGERS, WILMA ABELES. *Karl Kraus: A Viennese Critic of the Twentieth Century*. The Hague: Martinus Nijhoff, 1967.

————. "Karl Kraus and His Critics." *Modern Austrian Literature* 8, nos. 1 & 2 (1975): 26–47.

————. "Some Observations on Kraus's Impact Then and Now." In *Konkrete Reflexion, Festschrift für Hermann Wein*, edited by J. M. Broekman and J. Knopf, pp. 207–211. The Hague: Martinus Nijhoff, 1975.

JANIK, ALLAN, and TOULMIN, STEPHEN. "Language and Society: Karl Kraus and the Last Days of Vienna." In *Wittgenstein's Vienna*, pp. 67–91. New York: Simon and Schuster, 1973.

LILIENFELD, ROBERT. "Reflections on Karl Kraus." *The Nation*, 23 April 1973, pp. 534–537; 30 April 1973, pp. 568–573.

MENCZER, BÉLA. "Karl Kraus and the Struggle against the Modern Gnostics." *Dublin Review*, no. 450 (1950): 32–52.

NUNBERG, H., and FEDERN, E., eds. *Minutes of the Vienna Psychoanalytic Society, 1908–1910.* (Presentation of "The *Fackel* Neurosis" by Fritz Wittels, pp. 382–393.) New York: International Universities Press, 1967.

REICHERT, HERBERT W. "The Feud between Franz Werfel and Karl Kraus." *Kentucky Foreign Language Quarterly* 4 (1957): 146–149.

ROCKWELL, JOHN. "Offenbach . . . and Other Germans." *Opera News*, 10 April 1971, pp. 24–25.

ROSENFELD, SIDNEY. "Karl Kraus: The Future of a Legacy." *Midstream*, April 1974, pp. 71–80.

SIMONS, THOMAS W., Jr. "After Karl Kraus." In *The Legacy of the German Refugee Intellectuals*, edited by Robert Boyers, pp. 154–173. New York: Schocken Books, 1972.

SNELL, MARY. "Karl Kraus's *Die letzten Tage der Menschheit:* An Analysis." *Forum for Modern Language Studies* 4 (1968): 234–247.

SPALTER, MAX. "Karl Kraus." In *Brecht's Tradition*, pp. 137–155. Baltimore: Johns Hopkins Press, 1967.

STERN, J. P. "Karl Kraus's Vision of Language." *Modern Language Review* 61 (1966): 71–84.

———. "Karl Kraus and the Idea of Literature." *Encounter*, August 1975, pp. 37–48.

WILLIAMS, C. E. "Karl Kraus: The Absolute Satirist." In *The Broken Eagle: The Politics of Austrian Literature from Empire to Anschluss*, pp. 187–235. New York: Barnes & Noble; London: Elek, 1974.

ZOHN, HARRY. *Karl Kraus.* New York: Twayne Publishers, 1971.

————. "Karl Kraus: Prophet of Protest and Purity of Language." *Jewish Quarterly* 15 (1967): 34–36.

————. "A Crown for Zion: Karl Kraus and the Jews." *Wiener Library Bulletin* 24 (1970): 22–26.

————. "Krausiana: Karl Kraus in English Translation; Current Criticism of Karl Kraus." *Modern Austrian Literature* 3 (1970): 25–35.